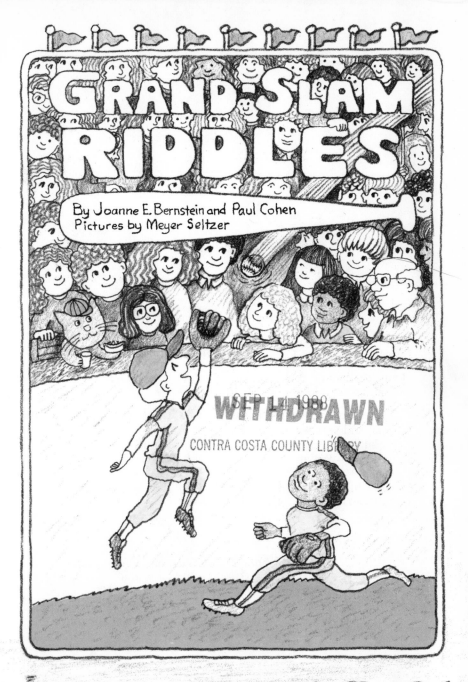

GRAND-SLAM RIDDLES

By Joanne E. Bernstein and Paul Cohen
Pictures by Meyer Seltzer

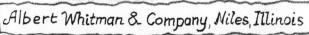

Albert Whitman & Company, Niles, Illinois

Library of Congress Cataloging-in-Publication Data

Bernstein, Joanne E.
  Grand-slam riddles.

  Summary: A collection of jokes and riddles about baseball teams,
players, and various aspects of the game.
  1. Riddles, Juvenile. 2. Baseball—Juvenile humor.
[1. Baseball—Wit and humor. 2. Riddles. 3. Jokes]
I. Cohen, Paul. II. Seltzer, Meyer, ill. III. Title.
PN6371.5.B3942 1988   818'.5402   87–25335
ISBN 0–8075–3038–7 (lib. bdg.)

To my favorite Yankee fan, Andy.
J.B.

To the Brooklyn Dodgers, who got me interested,
and to Tim McCarver, who keeps me interested.
P.C.

To Leo—friend, storyteller,
games-master . . . wizard for all seasons.
M.S.

Grandstand Giggles

What do you get if you borrow a player from Texas?
A Loan Ranger.

Who are the toughest fans?
The Toronto Boo Jays and the Milwaukee Booers.

Why didn't Dracula eat at the ball park?
The Count was full.

Why is the baseball championship not a laughing matter?
Because it's the World Serious.

Why was the piano tuner hired to play for the Red Sox?
He had perfect pitch.

Have you ever seen a house fly at the ball park?
No, but I've seen a home run.

| CAMELOT CRUNCHERS | 3 | 2 | 0 | 1 | | | | | | | R 6 |
| TURNBRIDGE TROLLS | 0 | 0 | 0 | | | | | | | | 0 |

Why does it take longer to go from second to third than from first to second?
Because between second and third there's a short stop.

When did King Arthur see baseball?
He attended knight games.

Why are Philadelphia fans tired of baseball?
They've had their Phil.

Where do they list baseball injuries?
On the scarboard.

What's the best place to keep the cowhide?
In the bull pen.

What do you call a stadium escalator?
A fan belt.

The Stars Come Out

When do you call Andre Dawson the wrong fielder?
When he's not the right fielder.

Why did people hate the Yankees after the Babe retired?
They'd become Ruthless.

Why will the Mets' Darryl have a long career?
Strawberry fields forever.

Why did Willie Mays's home runs travel so far?
They were "Giant" home runs.

Which outfielder is part of a car?
Dave Windshield.

Which Baseball Hall-of-Famer always has a cold?
Hankie Aaron.

What do the Oakland fans sing to Mr. Canseco before each game?
"José, can you see?"

Why did Goose Gossage go camping?
To pitch the tent(h).

Home Run

What's a batter's favorite delicatessen treat?
A grand salami.

Why did the batter bring a screwdriver up to the plate?
To drive a screwball, of course.

Who keeps the batter's box neat?
The cleanup hitter.

The Big Pitch

Why did the pitcher's watch stop?
He didn't wind up.

What candy bar scares pitchers?
Baby Ruth.

Which team's batters should be hit by pitches least often?
The Dodgers.

Why did the pitcher toss coins up in the air?
He wanted to throw his change-up.

LITTLE PITCHERS HAVE BIG EARS.

Why was the pitcher covered with ink?
He'd just come in from the pen.

What does a pitcher throw when he hasn't eaten all day?
A fast ball.

What's the pitcher's favorite candy bar?
Mounds.

Why was the teacher angry at the young pitcher?
He was throwing spitballs in class.

Calling Them as We See Them

What state do umpires come from?
New York. It's the umpire state.

What's the difference between an umpire and a pickpocket?
An umpire watches steals; a pickpocket steals watches.

Why are umpires so fat?
They're always cleaning their plates.

Baseball Cards

What does a runner on third base like to sing?
"There's no place like home."

Why did the catcher carry a hammer?
To nail runners to the plate.

What does the catcher sing to his mitt?
Glove songs.

Who plays for the Kansas City Royals and never wears a uniform?
The organist.

How should you compare two base runners?
Slide by slide.

Why did the Reds rookie have coal on his face?
He'd just come from the miners.

Where should you look for the San Diego chicken?
In fowl territory.

Why did the thirsty manager go to the bull pen?
For a relief pitcher.

How are an outfielder and a spider alike?
They both catch flies.

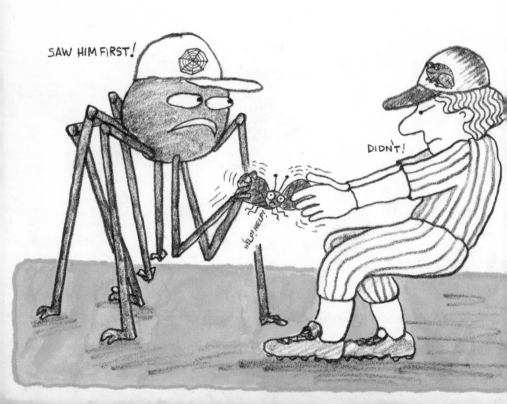

Beleague It or Not

Why don't the Dodgers play poker?
The Cards are in St. Louis.

What team is mentioned in the national anthem?
Atlanta, the home of the Braves.

What team goes best with milk?
The Baltimore Oreos.

What would the Toronto team be called if they moved to Milwaukee?
The Brew Jays.

What cars belong in the ball park?
Los Angeles Dodges.

What's the least expensive baseball team?
The Pirates; they're just nine "Bucs."

Which team can put nine dogs on the field?
The New York Mutts.

What do you call a twin bill in Montreal?
Double Expo-sure.

Why are the Blue Jays so good on the bases?
They always know where to-run-to (Toronto).

What do you call the Toronto team after a bad season?
The *very* Blue Jays.

Why are the Mariners so clean?
They go home to Wash.

What do the Cleveland Indians do when they don't succeed?
Tribe, tribe again.

What do you call an old Phillie?
A mare.

Why do the Houston Astros win so much?
Just dome luck.

On what team is it hardest to tell the players apart?
The Minnesota Twins.

By the Rules

What do you call nine runs in a team's first at-bat?
A big inning beginning.

What did the ambulance bring to the game?
The seventh inning stretcher.

Where do they tell tall tales about pitching?
In the bull pen.

AND THEN I STRUCK OUT THE SIDE, YEAH, AND THEN I WAS MVP, YEAH...AND THEN I...

What part of a baseball uniform lasts the longest?
The underwear—because it's never worn out.

How do we know that baseball players belong to unions?
They're often called out on strikes.

What insect gives his life to drive home a run?
The sacrifice fly.

What crime is encouraged in baseball?
Hit and run.

Why did the pitcher have rabbit for dinner?
He wanted to put more hop in his fast ball.

What do you call a pop-up during an evening game?
A fly by night.

Hall of Shame

Where is the baseball Hall of Shame?
In Blooperstown.

What television show features future Hall of Shamers?
The Game of the Weak.

What Hall of Shamer never got into a game?
Johnny Benched.

Diamonds and Other Gems

Where do fencing fans go for a ball game?
To Shea. (Touché.)

What type of snack would you bring to Wrigley Field in Chicago?
A Cubcake.

Which stadium has the most worms?
Wriggly Field.

Silly Statistics

The Detroit Tigers won 4 to 0, but not a single man touched first base. How was this possible?
They were all married men.

In another game the score was 13 to 0 although not one man reached base. How was *this* possible?
It was a woman's game.

Why did the girls' team have the most runs?
They wore cheap stockings.

What's the biggest jewel in the world?
A baseball diamond.

Extra Innings

What did the Montreal sportswriter write?
An Expo-say.

What do you call a pitcher who's thrown too many bean balls?
A has-bean.

What's the favorite cake in Anaheim?
Angel food.

What happens when Luke Skywalker screams about a decision?
The umpire strikes back.

Why did the shortstop bring a priest and a minister to the game?
For a double pray.

How do you make a baseball uniform last?
Make the glove and shoes first.

When do baseball teams honor good students?
On promotion days.

What has become of the team called the Dirty Sox?
They're washed up. Now they're the White Sox.

Why did the manager look in the cookbook?
For a better batter.

Have you ever heard a screaming line drive?
No, but I've seen a fly bawl.

If you were locked in a room with nothing but a baseball bat, how would you get out?
Take three strikes and you're out.

Why was the tax man in Los Angeles?
He was looking for Dodgers.

What did the chicken do at the plate?
He fowled one off.

What is the largest room in the losing team's clubhouse?
The room for improvement.

When is it coolest at Yankee Stadium?
When there are fans in every seat.

When the ball was swallowed by a pig in the outfield, what was the umpire's call?
"Inside the pork, home run!"

What dogs are welcome in the ball park?
Hot dogs.

Why is the Padres' chicken insulting?
He speaks fowl language.

What's the difference between a ball and a prince?
One is thrown to the air; the other is heir to the throne.

Why didn't the first baseman get to dance with Cinderella?
He missed the ball.